Practicing Yoga in a Former Shoe Factory

poems by

Heather Corbally Bryant

Finishing Line Press
Georgetown, Kentucky

Practicing Yoga in a
Former Shoe Factory

ACKNOWLEDGMENTS

"Our Mothers" originally published in *Fourth & Sycamore*, March 2018

"Walking Beside Lidian's Harp" originally published in *Old Frog Pond Farm Press
Plein Air Chapbook*, September 2018

"Biking, Luxembourg Gardens" originally published in *Compass Rose* (Finishing
Line Press, 2015)

"Crevices" originally published in *Cheap Grace* (Finishing Line Press, 2011)

"Lady Slippers on Pinnacle Road" originally published in *Cheap Grace* (Finishing
Line Press, 2011)

"Old Gambling House" published in *Cheap Grace* (Finishing Line Press, 2011)
previously published in the anthology, *In Other Words*, 2007

"At the Georgia O'Keefe Show, Ann Arbor" originally published in *Lottery Ticket*
(University of Wisconsin at Madison Libraries, Parallel Press Series, 2013)

Publisher: Leah Maines
Editor: Christen Kincaid
Cover Art: Photo Credit, HCB, with thanks to Spirit Bear Yoga Studio, Natick
Author Photo: Richard Howard
Cover Design: Elizabeth Maines McCleavy

Printed in the USA on acid-free paper.
Order online: www.finishinglinepress.com
also available on amazon.com

Author inquiries and mail orders:
Finishing Line Press
P. O. Box 1626
Georgetown, Kentucky 40324
U. S. A.

Table of Contents

For my children, for always

Hovering

When I floated above myself after giving
Birth—thinking it might be my last moment
On earth—my half life here—did I already

Have a near death experience and miss the
Meaning—if I ever need a lesson in being—
I can return to this moment of almost leaving—

I was peaceful, unafraid, and weirdly calm,
Hovering above the woman bleeding out on
The delivery table—looking down from the

Ceiling—wondering if she would be alright,
But also sure it didn't really matter then—she
Had delivered two new lives safe on earth—

I never want to forget that instant of pure
Being—the nurse who held my hand while she
Whispered in my ear that I might be having

Surgery soon—needles stuck in my shoulders,
Just in case—an oxygen mask smelled funny—
Even though I was thirsty, nothing to drink by

Mouth—days later when I came out of the haze,
I learned I almost lost my uterus, and also my life.

The Scream, November

I know that scream—it contains terror, anxiety, survival—
I have made that same sound, screamed in the same tone
Even when no one could hear me—the scream pierces

The silence all around us—please don't harm the children—
A mother interposing her body between her husband, eyes
Wild with rage and her own self—ready to take any hits

He will dole out—anything to spare the children—anything—
I couldn't get the pitch out of my head all day long—it stayed
With me, preyed on my mind—how can this violence persist,

This chokehold men have on women to make them so afraid?

Breathing Through My Life

Sometimes I realize I have not breathed
Deeply for quite some time—my chest
Has been rising and falling—but, like the
Shallows I can dip my toes in, my inhalations
Narrow—I remember a yoga teacher
Saying I need to see my chest moving—that
Is all—it always come back to breathing,
Doesn't it? That's how we know we are living.

Practicing Yoga in a Former Shoe Factory

Looking up, I see a white tin painted ceiling high above—
I seem to be floating far away—stencil vines arranged

In a pleasing pattern—it's all a matter of breathing, or so
The yoga teacher says—inhaling, exhaling, letting your

Mind rest—that is a place where I am not at my best—
Bringing hands to heart, then to chest—pressed, thumbs

Raised skywards—in the olden days, as I say to my students,
People did not need to take classes to learn how to rest—life

Was simply not that complex—work and then sleep—now we
Are not sure of the difference between the two—responsibilities

Follow us everywhere—I think of factory clocks tolling quarters
Of hours—time after time—now we cannot let our minds ease—we

Live in a cacophony of not enough peace, chaos you might say—
Namaste, we say, as in another time we might once have prayed.

People Are Fogging Up the Church Windows

When I was a child, we played a game to pass the time—
Here's the church, here's the steeple, open the doors

And see all the people—we would wiggle our thumbs
To let our friends see inside our hands—on this Saturday

In December, the church is filling—there's even an overflow
Area with a live video streaming—windows begin steaming—

And eyes are streaming—that avowed mixture of dignity and
Despair orchestrated at the death of someone dear—death

In our midst—killed by a deer—we recall, we reminisce, we
Look for signs of serendipity, messages from afar, remembrance—

The woman beside me says a medium told her it takes a while
For the departed to settle into an afterlife—when I look out

The windows again, the service has passed—rosy clouds tinge
A far and cold horizon—Daedalus is flying skywards, far above us

Racing Along Fenway, the View from the Back of an Ambulance

From the back of an ambulance, Boston skies rushed by—
December gray, and chill—I was no longer wearing my

Coat—in fact, I was not sure where my coat was—it's not
Often people take an ambulance from one hospital to

Another—I had been visiting my father in a rehabilitation
Facility when blood soaked through my maternity overalls—

I couldn't remember the last time I had felt my twins move—
Months away from my due date—I cradled my abdomen

As if in prayer—I whispered, please, please be alive in there—
But memory lapses at crucial junctions—I asked the attendant

If we could slow down, the twisting roadway of Storrow Drive
Was making me dizzy, the sound of our siren terrifying—we

Did not stop for a single light—we raced through them all—I
Asked again if we could slow down— instead, he pressed a cold cloth

On my forehead, and another one between my legs in an attempt
To stem the bleeding—I was worried about ruining my borrowed

Denim overalls—they had a polka dot pattern and were one of
The few articles of clothing I could still fit into—*placenta previa*

The EMT said—I couldn't even remember what that was—when
I asked, he asked me to close my eyes and breathe—we would

Be at the emergency room soon, where my doctor was expecting me.

On Probability and Other Matters

I never understood probability—and I wondered if this matter
Might sometime become a liability—perhaps I would have paid

More attention when the new math got rolled out—how the
Probability of choosing a blue block out of a sack of square

Blocks changed depending on how many blocks there were
Altogether—and also, how many chances you took—perhaps

I would have taken in more deeply the idea that is it fifty, or
Sixty percent of all first marriages fail as I learned in my mandatory

Divorce class in central Pennsylvania on a grim December day—
No grades given, only a survey at the end—sixty seven percent of all

Second marriages last—but the sweet spot seems to be the third
Time charmed when the percentage of success climbs into the

High eighties, or early nineties—perhaps memory fades as we
Celebrate age—my obstetrician held two apples in his hand as he

Explained to me the chances of one of my twins having, in his words,
A birth defect—I couldn't get it through my head on that scorching

June day in his office overlooking the Charles River that the likelihood of
Picking one bad apple, those were the words he said, doubles when you

Have two babies at the same time—I listened, incredulous, as he drew
A graph of the rising chances of risks, of the difficulty of bearing more

Than one baby at a time—he was arguing for an amniocentesis which
I was worried about having—because I did not want to lose a pregnancy

Like all the others I had worked so hard for—only later when I learned
How real the problems could be, did I relent to having the longest

Needle I have ever seen inserted deep inside my rounding belly—only
Then did I flinch, not at the pain, but at the realization of just how much

Risk I was undertaking—informed consent took on a whole new meaning.

America is Burning, Los Angeles August 11, 1965

America is burning, was what my father said to five-year-old me—
As we stood atop a hillside overlooking Los Angeles—

I could see big smoke bellowing and blowing
Far beneath but I couldn't make out any flames—

My father hoisted me atop his shoulders—so
I could see red, tangerine, and orange in the city below—

America is burning, he repeated, shaking his head,
America is burning and he wanted me to see the devastation

Hatred could cause—now we might say he was passionate
About social justice—he had seen first-hand what

Happened in Munich in 1933 when he attended one of
Hitler's rallies as an exchange student to see what the noise was

About—he came back afraid, afraid for the world, resigning
From his fraternity, afraid for what he saw coming—this

Morning when I read the news of hate crimes on the rise in
This country, I heard his voice saying, America is burning, again.

Our Mothers

For Rene and Marcella

Our mothers, we think, would have liked one another—
An unlikely pair, Marcella and Rene, though not really,

Over cigarettes and sherry, later only the sherry—they
Would have remarked on their doctor's elegance—it

Could take me over an hour to figure out what my mother's
Doctor had said about her obstructive lung disease instead

I heard that her doctor had been wearing elegant blank
Pumps, definitely by Armani—my mother liked that her

Doctor did not wear a white coat—your mother would have
Liked that too—but both Rene and Marcella would have

Been wearing short pearls, and sipping their sherry—
Would have turned to one another and said how happy

They were their daughters had become such good friends.

The Necklace

The scene when my daughter and I arrived was
Grim—my mother had been transferred to the

Nursing section of her assisted living facility—
Early October, almost my birthday—she'd been

Rolled into an ambulance from the apartment
She did not know she would never see again—

And so she deputized people to go back and
Find her most valuable possessions—her mind

Was vague, wandering—it was hard to believe
But she did not know where anything was—

She took me by surprise when she had my
Birthday present sitting in a small white box

On her lap in the wheelchair where she now sat—her
Whole body compressed with the notion that

At best, she was dying, just not already dead
Yet—her fingers fumbling, she apologized for

Not having time to find wrapping paper or a card.

The Ground Round, Lawrence, 1982

Maybe that's part of my poetry—to remember what other
People forget—maybe much of it is not of significance, merely

Fueling regret—I have regrets over you, regrets about the way
I treated you—I am relieved you have been kind enough to

Forgive me for a series of youthful mistakes as I was figuring out how
To make my way—I didn't know how any of it worked—but I

Do remember as I sit across from you on this mid-winter evening—
We ate dinner early then—at the Ground Round in Lawrence where

They served limitless popcorn with their hamburgers—it was a
March evening, and it was raining—I trusted losing my

Virginity to you—quaint I was, ridiculous, unschooled in the ways
Of the world—but you were patient, funny, and kind—this scene

Comes tumbling back into memory on this chilly December evening.

In Plain Sight

Where does hope reside—in my daughter's
Infectious smile, her laugh echoing through
The phone—in her brother's long strides—

His determination to make right all that he
Can—in my youngest son's humor—that's a
Non-starter, Mom—he'll say, in the kindest

Way—I have reclaimed my life in hope and
Peace—I have made room to let love in where
It can thrive again—broken promises leave us

Bereft—lies and attacks keep us defensive—
Disparage is a strong word—lies of omission
Can be just as harmful as sins of omission—

Once again, I am cast back onto my power to
Believe I can see what is already in plain sight.

To the Cemetery, Sleepy Hollow

No one else is here but me—at least as far as the eye
Can see—the cemetery is free, free for thought, free
Of visitors today—my parents here before me—

Through a crook in the Kousa dogwood, the one
In full bloom when my father died—I see their graves,
Names engraved, together again—although for a long

While it was only my father, until my mother joined
Him at last—she wanted to see him again—though I'm
Not sure what she believed in, if anything—today skies

Are filled with a heaviness of impending rain—full of
Early darkness and time for Thanksgiving—even the
Dogs are quiet here—I sit on the frozen ground, putting

Down my bag, planning to stay awhile—I chat with them—
Their two souls elsewhere—I will visit soon again, I say.

Waiting for my Daughter at the Providenciales Airport

I am waiting for my daughter in the Providenciales
Airport—just before Christmas when the air here

Has climbed past eighty degrees—several people
Ask if they can help me—I smile, shaking my head

And say I am waiting for my daughter to arrive—how
Long I wanted to be able to say those words, my

Daughter—how long until I knew I was carrying her—
By accident I learned she was a she, by a scary

Amniocentesis test I learned she was okay—
I learned she could do a flip turn inside me—after

Five hours of using up the free wifi, looking at
Rental cars lining a sandy hill—she walks through

The glass doors past customs, beaming—she is here.

The Caribbean Princess Docks, Middle Caicos

My daughter and I arrive a half hour early to meet
The Caribbean Princess, as the outfitted ferry is called—
Hoping her brothers are on it—first time we have all

Been together in a year—and it is a mother's dream to have
Her flock together—just being with each other and having
The time to know one another again, to be friends, to

Remember what it feels like for all of us to be together—
At the beginning, I am too excited to sleep—by the end I'm
Counting down the days contained in memories and

Pictures, pictures to get me through the new year—I
Turned around and my children grew up—look, my
Daughter says—look, there they are—waving at us

From the ferry as it pulls into the slip, secured by rope.

Walking Whitby Beach with my Daughter

We have been walking beaches together
Since before you can remember—for us,
It is a time to be unfettered, free, and in the

End, these talks between you and me cover
Everything—we exchange the mysteries of
A woman's life—passages no one else

Would ever understand—and we wish, in
Glorious gratitude, for times like this—times
When we can pass along the secrets of a

Lifetime—I hope some of my scars will show
You how to live differently—I hope, in turn,
That you will show me how to make my way

To a healthy kind of loving, the reciprocal kind.

The Trigger Fish Gets a Talking to

Sean, the fisherman, does not like these fish—they
Swarm our little ship—he curses and swears—
The females fare somewhat better than the

Males—he believes in corporal punishment,
At least for the fish—because he whacks the
Black and purple fins against his boat's edge

Before tossing them back—leaving the lucky
Ones confused circling, trying to orient
Themselves in these turquoise waters—some

Of the less fortunate ones end up on their back,
Eyes open, like T.S. Eliot's Phoenician—I fear
For their death, their wantonness, she-devils

He calls them, get a talking to—like his wife.

Bottle Creek Landing, North Caicos

On Christmas morning life is harsh here—
Behind the bright pinks, greens, and yellows
Of tourist beacons, in the hollows—the

Underside life we are not supposed to
See—rusted out trucks, junked in groves of
Scrub, boarded up windows where hurricanes

Have blown through, piles of cement where
Housing starts have been made and then
Abandoned as investors have discussed their

Plummeting value around a table in New York,
Evaluating their prospects—meanwhile at Bottle
Creek Landing, an elderly gentleman emerges

From his truck to wash his gangrened foot in
The warm waters swirling in this creek—who

Ever said life was anything remotely fair.

Cemetery, Bambarra Beach

The land is bare here, soil thin, scrub low—
And you know the graves must be shallow,
Beside Bambarra Bay lies a small inlet, a

Quick passerby might miss—the graves are
Raised which makes me wonder if they could
Float away in a heavy rain, or a category four

Hurricane—as we look close, we see duct tape,
Mounds of artificial flowers piled high—maybe
That's for the man who died the same night

Emmanuel gave us a ride—our bodies floating
To the surface—yet we swim with the
Caribbean Sea, lying on our backs, thinking of

Those blocks of cement that kept the bodies
Below ground—kept them in hell—maybe it's
Just a heaven we haven't known yet.

Snow on Trees, Driving to New York in Five Degrees

Driving to Manhattan on this icy morning, wind chill
Has a feel of ten below, sun crisp on new snow—reminds
Me of the last drive to see my mom—I didn't know if

She would be speaking, or whether her eyes would have
Been open—yet there she was, after snow on trees—eyes
Closed, barely there, but she did grasp my hand like the

Almost dead Phoenician, Pisces that she was—I stayed
Inside for three days, in her bed almost all the time—until
I walked into sunshine to cross a street and buy coffee—

Chill air blew across my face and it was then I knew I
Was going to lose her soon, her grasp was fading—one
Night I slept with her into the morning when she was gone.

Day of Epiphany, Manhattan

My friend and I rush from warmth to warmth,
The cold freezing our toes—one too many trips
Outside—and you are always on my mind—

I glance at my phone only to see those words we
First said to one another decades ago—it was also
In the winter, January, I think—and clear, just like

This night in the city where buildings etched in ice rise—
Empire State lights turn white—in this first
Week of a new year when walking on your streets,

Waking on these early winter mornings reminds me of you.

Ice Melt, Red Wine, and Bacon

You bring me gifts: ice melt, laughter, happiness—
My front door is frozen shut, my steps impassable,
But it doesn't matter—it's all good, as we say now—

We are both nervous—after all it has been thirty-
Six years—the previous century—since we were
Last alone together—ice melt is for housewarming,

Wine for laughing—we talk so long it takes me over
An hour to cook the bacon—perhaps most of all you
Have brought me the gift of truth—to know what

I feel and to be able to say it too—to you—how warm
You are, how gentle—how sweet you taste in this love.

A Fire Storm

When I think of the words, they fly through
My mind, electric and crackling, one after
The other, a story begins to come to me,
Best as I can see, sitting in this quiet space,
I imagine a whole world, people marching
Through it—and I begin to know what I was
Put here on earth to do—after so many false
Starts, I was to tell the story right from my
Heart, all those years of wandering have
Brought me back to where I wanted to be
For the first time—in my mind now,
I know which way I need to turn.

Three Poems for Us

Late March

When I met you for the first
Time on a cloudy morning in
March I saw a flash of your ring—
You were young, I thought,
To be married—and cute too,
But what did I know about love
And marriage then—I knew you
Were off limits, thus I proceeded
With caution—I believe we shook
Hands after the interview, before
I watched you walk away—I in
My pleated gray skirt and plain
Raspberry sweater purchased
For an interview at a bank for a
Job I neither wanted nor was given—

Sometime in October

I remember the strangest details—
The party at your house was for
Halloween—your then wife
Fascinated me—she was dark
And beautiful and she wore tall
Boots that made her look cool—
I had just turned twenty-two—
How little I knew of love—I had
Managed to graduate from college
A virgin—that night, I either remember
Or imagine you walked me to the door.

Early January

When we came back to school
That winter, people said your wife
No longer lived with you—that

Was all I knew—pretty soon, we
Were eating dinner with friends—
Your ring had disappeared, I knew
Not where—I was delighted to be
Spending time with you—we
Watched TV on your enormous set in an
An empty living room and before long, we
Were going to the movies—you always
Held the door for me—and eating Chinese
Food, walking across campus in the
Afternoons, mornings came too soon.

Mid-Seasons

I.

By April I was in love with you—I
Yearned to be your lover—on that
Rainy spring evening we ate popcorn
At the Ground Round—you knew I
Was terrified and were so gentle—
Later I worried about having got
Blood on your sheets—you reassured
Me—I was convinced I would be bad
At sex—yet, with you, somehow I wasn't—
Through all the years I kept track of you—
Every now and then, you turned up in a dream
Or two—a poignant reminder of what might have been—

II.

But on that
December evening as I sensed you
Watching me, I knew something had
Changed—something had been
Rearranged—I didn't dare to hope—
But there it was, you felt it too—now we
Are young and old together at the same
Time—the us who were, the us who
Might have been, the us we are becoming.
It is as though each of our lives has
Folded into the other, so we exist both
In the finite past and the indeterminate
Future—the miracle is that we can know
Both now—who we were and who we are—
With thirty-six years stretching in between—
Everything is old and new, a lifetime of knowing.

On Keel Beach, Achill Island

Why not say what happened?
    –Caroline Blackwood, *Great Granny Webster*

I.

We were so young then—I twenty-one and you, a mere
Twenty-six when we fell in love—sweet green afternoons,
Cut grass wafted through your wide-open windows.

II.

We drank beer and jumped off a pier at Squam Lake—we
Stayed up all night before the solstice wondering if we
Were star-crossed lovers—my parents disapproved—

III.

You were not yet divorced—I was torn between heart and
Mind—we stayed up late reading Yeats, Hemingway, Fitzgerald,
Carol Muske-Duke, Robert Fitzgerald, and Andre Dubus—

IV.

You told me I would be a good teacher, maybe a writer too—I
Was easily dissuaded, persuaded by others—I broke up with
You in a cruel letter, posted from Oxford, the one letter I wish

V.

I'd never sent—when it arrived, you told you me played *Always on
My Mind*, over and again, a record turning on a table, telling me
I broke your heart—later I would understand I had broken my

VI.

Own heart as well, but I didn't know that then—a lifetime
Between what we once knew and what we later understood—on
The day of your divorce, you called me from a payphone at the

VII.

Salem Courthouse—I didn't know what to say—three and
A half decades later we remembered what was once said and what
Could not be unsaid—you sent me a dozen red roses to my office—

VIII.

I blushed on their arrival—I was too young or foolish, or both, to
Know what real love was and so we left it—we both went on to
Inhabit other lives until we again remembered our sweet

IX.

Young love—the way mowed grassed smelled on June afternoons—
I sent you poems, you answered them—I divorced, then you—we
Danced around each other, too unsure to trust again, to begin anew,

X

Until that mid-December evening when we met at Lemon Thai and
Laughed the restaurant closed—and you watched me walk to my
Car—until you showed up with one rose and ice melt at my door.

On the Old Cork Road

All morning the rain and sun have alternated, shadows shifting
Across the Ballyhoura Mountains—and I've thought of you all
Along the way, of how I wrote about you long ago—and used

The word infinite—in Ireland, infinity of time is everywhere—
People stop to chat, lunch lasts hours, a cuppa tea could take
An afternoon—there are no pennies, expanses stretch green

Everywhere along this drive—we dip down into deep hollows,
Ditches along roadsides, horse-drawn hay carts having passed
Before us—rhododendrons, ferns, and snowdrops line the route—

Daffodils are sprouting here, through the rich soil, moss covers
Limestone—there was snow in Dublin when the plane touched
Down—and I thought of you sleeping when I was waking, and

I yearned to be lying next to you again—as we had been before,
And before that too—I wanted to send the whole rainbow to you.

The Laws of Physics Do Not Explain Everything

We are lying in bed after making cosmic love—ours
Is not to reason why, why it is so good between
Us—perhaps there is too much to be understood—

Some laws do not explain everything, you say, like
How one thing can affect the movement of another
Thing—even when the two objects are not touching,

Are not even in close proximity—we are lying in
Bed after making love—just as I turn on my left
Side to go to sleep, you reach your warm hand to

Cup my body, to let me know that you are there,
That in ways neither of us understands, in fact,

You have always been there, as have I.

The Onion

I.
Here are some words I don't know how to say aloud:
I am like an onion, the food that scares me maybe
Because I am so much like it—my layers go deep—

I have been threatened, taunted, mocked, debased,
Raped—all in the name of love—I have been told I was
Crazy, stupid, foolish, fat, and lazy—I have been lied

To, cheated, given the silent treatment, slapped, pushed
Against a wall, shoved out of a moving car in Michigan—
Told that I would never be loved again—I have been left

When I was bleeding to death, dropped off at the
Hospital to find my way, I have been told that I was the most
Beautiful woman on earth, also the ugliest woman in the

Universe, that I was brilliant, impossible, dumb, selfish—
Told that I was perfect, told that I was complete dirt—

II.
That I was unlovable; I have been left many times, once at a
McDonalds in North Carolina with three tiny children and no
Wallet for more than an hour—have been told I wouldn't

Even be a good nanny, that I couldn't do anything right, that
My PhD was wasted on me, my dissertation a fiction—so please
Forgive me telling you of my secret history—it has left me

Feeling ashamed, foolish, filled with shame, completely lost
In the universe—sometimes—so please forgive me as I blunder
My way back—my abuse was secret, no one else knew—there

Was always another woman waiting in the shadows, someone
Who could jump in one instant to fill my shoes—forgive me for
Being sometimes confused as I make my way back to belief,

To certainty, to a love that is whole and pure and new and true—
That is what I am learning for the first time in my life with you.

Strawberry Moon

The Algonquin tribes named this huge

Moon in June the strawberry moon,

Because its appearance signaled it was

Time to pick the strawberries, this third

Moon in June, time to pick the ripening

Fruit sweet and tumbling into June, the

Fruit I made into jam to pass the time while

I waited to see if a baby was growing inside

Me—as it turned out, there was not one but

Two—it was the moon of the summer of

Bounty—the moon of beautiful ripening

Babies—growing deep, far inside me.

Walking Beside Lidian's Harp

Just past the waterfall—which for some strange reason I don't recall—
The path curves past a circle of sacred stones—all elements of creation
Abide here, among the deepest spirits of centuries—just before a path leads to

Forest, the grass is long, the earth dry, even with recent rain—almost a whole
season has turned since I walked here before—our earth has spun, circled on its
Head—just before turning into the glade, I sit and contemplate in shade—I feel

At home again here—earth, music, water, sphere—beauty carved out of a tree
In memory, then bronzed and gilded to span ages—in memory of a woman, a
Woman carved out of history—women creating, making, ultimately being—a
place of

Kinship for all those who may have been left aside in history—here is a place
For all those who wish to worship nature—an oasis—we can barely hear the
Distant thrum of highway, no jet trails today, only pure blue sky—just as earth
Has turned

A revolution, so I have I—this place calls to me, asking to be free, freed from
The tyranny of cruelty, freed from false beliefs in what constitutes love hereafter.

Migraine

All day I've fought a storm inside my own mind,
What lies in there that I cannot find; there is
Black and there is white and there are lights more
Bright than I would like in the night. I feel the strain
Of the emotions of others thrust upon me, I cannot
Push them away—I know a headache will come
To pass; it could not be otherwise; I take disappointment,
Sorrow, and all else inside myself, listening to voices
No one else can hear, I sit in the dark and swallow
Two blue pills. With them, I know, peace will come,
And then tears as my soul tries to right itself, to
Understand, best it can, what has come to pass.

Biking, Luxembourg Gardens

My friend meets me by the velo stand—
She has mastered the system—we charge
Our cards and remove our bikes—

A Saturday in August, everyone except
The tourists are leaving Paris—the streets
Are empty, just some passing cars, a few trucks—

We bike down the steep hill from Montmartre
Along the boulevards, past the Louvre, beside
The plane trees which give us much necessary

Shade until we end up by fountains in the
Luxembourg Gardens—we buy cappuccinos
From the small stand by reflecting pool

Where young boys and girls float their toy boats—
We mostly have the garden to ourselves—
The hot sun begins to rise higher before we

Begin our climb back—she is teaching me how to be,
At any given moment, simply in one place
And time: early one August morning in Paris.

Accidentals

In musical phrasing, these signs demarcate a
Note inhabiting an unexpected place on the
Scale, a stranger, an outlier, an anomaly,
Something out of the ordinary, a sound plucked
Out of its context—as in daily living,
Surprises startle us away from our everyday
Chores to twist what we think might happen,
Sometimes to trip us up; we learn, then, to
Anticipate the unfamiliar, the unexpected:
It is not what we do with the familiar
Which defines us, but how we behave when
We come across that which we do not know
That to which we cannot supply the answer,
We must bend and make new amends.

Crevices

Like ochre lichen growing in crevices between
Rocks, a woman's art seeds itself, choosing private
Spaces, places hidden from ordinary view—offering
A glimpse of beauty among what must
Be accomplished in the everyday.

Artists of the past—Emily Dickinson, Virginia
Woolf, Mary Cassatt—they had no children,
Sometimes neither husband nor lover either;
They were left each day with a blank canvas,
The white paper where they inscribed their rage,

Recording what was glorious to them,
And also most dangerous; I remember Yeats's dictum—
Perfection of the life or the art, one must choose—
One but not the other; I call to mind waves crashing
On rocks, water receding without noise,

Rushing, swirling, following ocean's force—
Its retreat opening fissures in rock, gaps between
Liquid and solid, stone and water—the most barren
Of all settings on earth where one spot of lichen
Brightens yellow and green after low tide.

Lady Slippers on Pinnacle Road

Cypripedium Acaule

Along curving roads we walk,
Pressing on towards orchards
Spreading over hillsides, green
Now, making fruit and leaves for
Summer shade; stone walls line
Old fields marking boundaries
Where land has been won, lost,
Sold and fought over—

It has rained for a week but
Today the air begins to lighten,
As though it needs not hold so
Much moisture anymore—

A small verdant patch of wild grass
Grows up a ways from the road,
Dew glistens on tall blades; three
Lady Slippers sprout up, perfectly
Formed, jaunty, tender, their
Blossoms elegant on rigid stems,
Pink globes of brightness,
Guardians protecting our path.

Gibbous Moon

Round white paper lantern hanging
Behind a trail of pink clouds, like
Feathers spread out from a pillow,
As twilight comes, clouds pass,
Turning to lavender cheer until
They've fled stage right.

Moon rises high and fast;
By supper's end, twilight has
Fallen, crepuscular and thin,
Not a speck of down remains, just
One big round satellite presides,
Phoebus in her gibbous phase

Pine Barren

Perhaps not one of you sees the
Transparency of the line for me
Between reality and insanity,
How close I am some days to
Crossing over into another
Country, a place of needles,
Hospital walls, gauze—I don't
Know how it got a start in me—
That trip when I was three,
The closed doors, the locks on
Intimacy—but all too soon I
Learned I was not to be
Affirmed, that crazy making
Line between petted like a dog
And then showed off, for being
In the way—all my life it's been
True, I've fought for what I knew,
What I could hold, know, or keep
To myself where no one lies to
Me, or tells me tales of things
Which I knew could only be
Otherwise—how hard I fought to
Become someone who could hold
Onto something that was mine, a
Way of understanding, but instead,
The pain came from all around—
Before I fought to be a mother—
It will only be the others who get in
The way—and then I must say no,
Here is what I believe, what I know.

Winter Berries

Wintering over, it's called, these brown
Sticks waving valiantly in the brisk
Wind, their last red berries
Lingering, luxuriating in their
New-found light; I collect as
Many as I might, knowing that
Their last blast of fire will keep
Me warm, hold some brightness
When heavy snows come.

The Bradford Pear Trees, September 2005

Even the fruit trees are confused—having lost their leaves,
Had them ripped off in high winds,

They think it's spring—they've started blooming all over again—
Either too early, or too late, however you may see it—

Bursts of soft white blossoms have sprung onto their branches,
Perhaps pears will come before winter, before anyone is ready—

Least of all the trees—
The rest have stood in high water, their roots soaked for no one knows

How long—it is questionable whether they will live—
This territory is all new, accountable, as we struggle to settle,

To stop the flood, to sweep away the debris,
We see how futile our searches may be.

Red Dragonfly

Bright red insect hovering over chartreuse-green grass—
Whining, swooping, suddenly still, as if taken by
Surprise on this blue September day—

As if by chance we met, and I looked hard at every
Line and wing—

The same way words tumble from my pen—
Until I etch and scratch against the paper—
Fixing them until my mind is freed to fly.

Queen Anne Cherries

Round globes of fruit, sweet to the center,
Firm case, stem where it had been once
Connected to the vine, should it have been so,
Orbs of plenty, beauty, strong, plum-wine colored
Strong in summer harvest, towards the middle
Of July, pink hearts of sweetness; you bite in
Through the skin, pit come out clean,
Plucked to the touch, tart, multi-hued,
Speckled red and white inside, in sheer
Loveliness, we start—I see a hill of trees
In bursts of May flower, you make the purity
Of the first, to taste, to enjoy, to savor,
To linger over as we feel just who
We might be on our way to becoming.

Holly Bushes

Holly hedges bloom with pinpricks
Of vermilion, sticky branches
Wind their way, needing to be
Tamed—a row of blue spruces
Grown tall, below yet more
Trees, pear I think, still full
With copper leaves bearing
The shape of their fruit—

Morning mist thickens,
Descending into valley,
The edges of our terrain wedged
Into a hilly crevice, part of
The Appalachian chain,
Sharp rocks rising out of soil
Where I begin again.

Crossing the Ridge

Late on a Monday night in December, the skies at ten
Thousand feet are pretty dark—just a few lights casting
Upwards from the valley—from above, the town looks
Contained, whole, complete; even from the window seat
Of an airplane clouds descend, too thick to penetrate—
When the pilot announces we will be landing soon, and the
Flight attendant will be dimming the cabin to prepare
For arrival—we may encounter some turbulence,
So we should not be surprised when this small metal shell
Bumps and halts, catching slightly all the way down.
To the ground until it stops in the shudder of taxiing.
In twelve hours, I have gone from here to there and
Back again—when I walk down steps to the tarmac,
The main terminal is closed so I take a side entrance to
The parking lot where I left my car—on the drive home
I think about what I will say to my husband and children
About what my mother's doctor told me that morning.

Eucharist, St. Andrew's Episcopal Church

On this chilly Christmas Eve, the first since you moved out,
I take my daughter and my youngest son to attend
The service of Eucharist—sitting in the cold, at the back
Of an Episcopal Church where we have never been—
We seek whatever comfort we might find on this holiest
Of nights—we each ponder in our hearts the knowledge that
We will never be a family together again, that my husband,
The father of my children, has irretrievably broken his vows
Honoring the sanctity of our marriage—in shock, sadness,
And a strange relief, the three of us mumble the words
To the Lord's Prayer almost silently, as though no one
Else should hear our cries of pain on this sacred and silent night
Celebrating the savior—on our way out we shake hands
With the minister, still filled with the aroma of incense and myrrh.

On Passing Some Black-Eyed Susans

As I was driving through Michigan, my eyes
Lit upon a patch of Black-Eyed Susans,
Their ochre colored petals tipping upwards,
Uneven toward the sun-burnt sky, their hue
A deepened yellow, buttery mustard, closer really
To tangerine, tall stems leafed out as wide as could
Be, pistons pulling light back into the blossoms'
Core since black is not the absence of
Refraction but the absorption of it; this crop
Planted beside a field of corn, just past season,
Luxurious, ebullient, joyful as the autumnal palette
Flares out in this last spectacle of brightness.

Hurricane Isabel

Gale winds tore at the thin land,
Tides raged against the fragile
Beaches, leveling the dunes,
Making Pepsi machines come
Flying by. A whole turquoise
Hotel came loose, unmoored,
Floating into air, until it
Came to rest diagonally atop a
Swimming pool. Beach chairs
Hurtled toward parking lots,
Houses sank into their pilings,
Bottomless pits opened up
Beneath the paved surfaces, as if for
A whole afternoon, the island
Had been tipped, topsy turvy,
World without end.

Cookie Tins and Roller Blades

When I think back on those crazed June days just past
The solstice when you first turned our life upside down
And then righted it again, your professed desire was
Premised on a series of partial truths, leading me to
Operate in a daze out of fear of losing the life we

Had, I thought, worked so hard to build—our children
Were young and I will never know why it was you
Wanted to parade your paramour in front of us, as if
To say, you better be careful or I will not stay—
Marriage is not an auction where the prize goes to

The highest bidder, but instead an endeavor based
On love and trust, perhaps most of all kindness—I
Have paid dearly to learn the extent of your infidelity—
And as I was walking beside you in the store, buying
Possessions for home and hearth, you were already

Plotting how you could slip the next lie from your tongue.

A School Room in Baghdad

Even here, violence spreads—it happens, children
Leave their parents in the morning to begin a day
Of study—they are reciting the alphabet when
The shelling begins, unrelenting, driving them under
Their desks; they take cover, hide and run—if they
Don't come in the first place, then education will
Lose out again; I wonder, not for the first time,
Just what we are all doing here, if anything.

A mother waits for her son and daughter at the end
Of the day, only this time, she holds her breath not
Once, not twice, but three times for luck—there,
At the end of a dusty lane, she sees them
Walking towards her.

Night Swimmer

Darkness softens under harsh brightness of fluorescent light:

Night comes tumbling over our humid universe—

Popsicles, hot dogs, pink cotton candy sweet—

Shouts come for the competitors—my daughter—

Strong, young, and confident swims to the finish

Line every time, pushing her hardest to touch first;

I think she will be racing for a long while—

Each instance, I know, she does her very best—

I hope she will be able to break away and have her

Way, at least most of the time, as she finds her

Path through this world; not much is going to stand

Between her and the places she wants to go;

On this sultry July evening, she pushes through turquoise water—

All that she learns will stay; crickets chirp tonight.

Old Gambling House

Way out in Pimlico Sound, a wooden
House stands on stilts, listing slightly
To the east; wind, rain, salt, and have
Battered it crooked, but it's still mostly
Intact—good old boys come here to drink,
Play cards, and bet money, just far enough
From shore to evade the police; there's
Something romantic about the idea of a tree
Fort built with nothing but water and tide,
The passage of long years; many a good time
Having been had here, girls lured out
To see the fun, raising plastic glasses at
Sunset, before the rise of full moon.

Springing Your Trap

Like a rabbit with my hoof caught in the trap you set
For me, I didn't know how to set myself free from
Your tangled reasoning, your mean figuring of how
You could keep me captive—you always counted
On me to stay with you, no matter what—

Here now in the middle of my life I stood up and dragged
My foot away from the prison you had made of
My days—you said I always had to live, no matter what—
In the jail you constructed from the duplicity of your
Beautiful words, your reliance on my naivety—

My dependence, my fear of being on my own—you relied
On winning me over, keeping me as prey to the terrible
Allure of self-destruction—you would tell me I was
Nothing without you, that I could not last a minute
Without you—and one glorious September day I knew that,

No matter what, I had to yank my bleeding foot away.

Eight Minutes Past Midnight

It has begun raining hard—I tell myself, when the weather
Turns, I will know my father has died—still, he holds on and
Through to another day—when the doctor ordered the breathing
Machine turned off, he predicted only a few more hours, a very few—
But I have allowed myself to go back to sleep and am deep under
When the telephone rings by my bedside—by the time I answer
It, I have forgotten what I am waiting for: I hear the voice of a
Stranger whose name I don't know—he tells me the sad news; he
Is sorry, he says; I hang up.

From our living room, where my mother is staying, I hear the
Screams, wails so deep I cannot fathom the noise, my mother's
Cries—before I can go downstairs, there are some things I have
To know—I dial the number of the hospital one last time—did he
Go peacefully or not, was he at odds, was he awake, did he sleep?
No one can tell me, they do not know what happened at the end—
But they do have one more question for us—can they do some
Research on his artificial hip—can they remove it from his body?

Thanksgiving Baby

Many years ago, on this day I learned
I was carrying a child—we celebrated
By roasting our first turkey, a marital
Milestone, and drinking chilled
Champagne with our friends—
It was just a tiny spot on a black and
White picture, deep inside me—I felt
Only the pureness of happiness, and
A refusal to see what might go wrong—
Instead, I closed my eyes and thought
Of what would come to pass, of the
Vows we'd said, of what we'd come
To believe—

On the first of December, we learned
Of a death—sometime over those few
Days, a tiny heart had failed to flutter.

Beslan School

The place which was before only a tower, with a school
And a church and a market square has become associated
With a sort of horror we despise—nor can we even
Surmise what might have happened there when Russian
Troops stormed a school filled with children, and looked
At them as though they had no care, then shot them
With impunity.

Forever more the name will only mean slaughter,
The murdering of the innocent as we let our hatred
Run amuck in the destruction of those who cannot
Bleed for them—as though there could be
Any satisfaction in such a tragic victory; not one of
Them is free, nor now can they ever be—only members
Of a terrible moment in history.

Near Mosul

A suicide bomber came at lunch, strapped explosives
Onto himself and walked into an army mess tent; the
Spoons were just beginning to scrape the pewter bowls.

In the end, nineteen soldiers died, one of the biggest
Casualty days of the war, except that we don't really
Call it a war anymore; it's an armed conflict, an operation,

A fight for freedom. I turn the face of the newspaper down;
I don't want the kids to see how very much is wrong with
This world they are learning to inhabit—how can

It be otherwise, how can there be so much harm in this
Dark place—in the smallest corners, I look for a note of
Grace, a promise of redemption for the evils we have
Been given, for the wrongs that we cannot possibly right.

Parents' Night, Middle School

The cafeteria is dark and quiet tonight, as we enter
And slip into the rows of chairs set up for us—
Someone turns on the light, and the principal
Begins to speak—there are slides for us to watch—
Our children need to wear sneakers, to remember
Their lunch money, and to finish their homework.

Lest we worry, they will learn other things here too—
Spelling, arithmetic, states and capitals, history will
All come to life—they will do a project on the National
Parks in the spring, canoe down a river in May, and
Spend the night in a tent; we should let them begin
To struggle to find their own answers.

They will be studying complex math, details of grammar
In language arts, going into more depth in social studies—
There will be specials too—as parents, we might not
Hear as much from you on your return from school
As we used to—in the car, you turn your cheek away from
Me when I try to kiss you good-bye in the morning—

The teacher reassures us that is all to be expected—
Sixth grade is the first break, a taste of the adolescence
To come—still, your skin feels soft and young—you
Will prepare me, as you have before, for what will
Come as we each make our separate ways in the world.
Backpack flying, you rush out the door—in this instant

I know I will never see you again as you are on this day.

The Huntress

I draw a circle around my body,
Like a shield you say, where
She cannot come in; here is
My life, where the story begins.

I wish it could be otherwise
That we could talk of whatever
It is that daughters speak
About to their mothers.

But you want more of me
Than there is to give, more
Than you can take; more than
You ever had a right to ask.

Orchards Burning

A puff of smoke crosses the sky—
Walking past, we see the new green
Coming now, rows of stubs, stumps,
Trees cut down, apple wood piled high.

Blue stretches tight—the road turns,
We linger, looking at bonfires
Gathering steam, flames shooting
Out wildly now over the fields.

Neighbors talk of the changes that
Are bound to come in time; there is
Always a builder lurking nearby,
Threatening to bulldoze orchards
And pave the land with houses.

Fetal Demise

A few years ago now, I mourned
The start of a life I was trying
To grow shakily in my uterus—
Until I saw a tiny heartbeat
Fluttering—there you were, oh
Nameless one.

But as I watched, the rate
Lowered, halted, started up
Again—something was not
Right, as I discovered in the
Middle of the night.

Back at the hospital the next
Afternoon, a lonely sac
Remained, drained of a
Heart beat; as I drove home
In the twilight, I cried for
What was simply not to be.

Fallujah

Place names pop up, specks across the globe—
Some of them we've heard before, some of them
Are new to us—Marines lost, trucks jumped, dead
Bodies bagged, loaded into the back—one man,
Maniacal, says nothing will stop us; right is on
Our side. He will entertain no other plans.

We celebrate Easter, the coming of rebirth
Amidst shouts of hate; the cries grow louder
Still, for revenge, justice, a ceasefire; meanwhile,
Politicians split hairs over whether any one of
Them could have seen this coming; hairs caught
In a microscope, all too easily noted in retrospect.

Grave Digger

White truck pulls up alongside
A big hole in the earth: the
Ceaseless rains break clouds,
Still looming dark and gray.

A man wields a shovel, heaping
And piling dirt into the back
Of his bed, soon the heap will be
Higher than he, and he will be done.

He stands in the middle of the
Hole in the earth, halfway
Submerged, the job finished—
He looks up at the sky and smiles.

Time to go home for dinner.

Lilacs

Early in May, lilacs come through,
New and purple, softened by sun,
A huge bush of them sprinkles color
And beauty down a whole block—

There, just for the asking, outside
The fence. A woman waits for the
Bus, scarf pulled up against her
Neck, bracing for the lingering chill—

Still, no one is looking; she peers
Around, and glances to see who
Might see. For the moment, at least,
She is ostensibly alone on the street—

Surreptitiously, she reaches her hand
Up through the greenery, wrapping
Her fingers around a wad of
Aubergine blossoms, pulling as
Hard as she can, she breaks off
One glorious branch to take home.

Squannacook River

Here river swirls, eddies, pushes right past us—
We set out with the hope born of any human
Experience—preparation, explanation, launch—
You sit up at the head of the canoe, my paddling
Partner to be; we see Red-Winged Blackbirds,
A pair of Baltimore Orioles, beaver scent
Mounds, establishing territory and attracting
Mates; best of all, we spot one Great Blue Heron

Flying over us all in a moment of silence, all is calm.
We close our eyes, listen to the sounds of water, bird,
Faraway bulldozer, frog—on the way back, we
Pass seven painted turtles splayed on sunny rocks—
With the wind at our backs, we make good time.

At the Georgia O'Keefe Show, Ann Arbor

Your colors swirl around—black, white, green, orange,
And purple—you paint a vision for us all to see—
Villages, hills, rooftops turned to designs and
Shapes all around, a river squiggles and squirms
Through a canyon red and yellow—western, eastern
Views, rocks to clouds hanging above blue sky
Veiled in spots of white and clear and swept away—

That is what I want to be able to do—to show you how
I see the world, clear painted view, plainly—so that
Nothing will stand in my way here on this mountaintop.

What if Beowulf Had Been Written by a Woman

Something I wondered just the other day—
What if Beowulf had been inspired by a woman's
Tale—what if a woman were the primary scribe

And mastermind—would that have changed the
Course of literary history—or would everything
Have been the same anyway—in the old narrative

Men wrote books, women cleaned counters—what
If we could know her name—would that have made
Any difference? Or would we still be reading books

By men pretending to know how women work?

Winter Sunday Afternoon, Your Driveway

That moment in the car—a winter Sunday
Afternoon—a lifetime in a heartbeat of
Extraordinary moments—you in the most

Ordinary of ways were about to pull into
Reverse—you paused, and I knew exactly
What you were going to say—before you

Said it—most uncanny now—we each know
What the other is going to say—and it could
Not be any more delicious, or unexpected,

But somehow not—I have spent the rest of
This January day feeling full with gladness,
Hope, and love—after all we have come back

To what matters most, after all—this is us.

Eating Lunch at Commons, February

If we can know our former selves, then
We can remember why we were together—
And we will never know if we would have

Broken up in between—but that doesn't
Really matter now—I have twinges of
Remembrance and forgetting—as I think

Of that winter, and spring and almost
Summer we spent together—the olden
Days as our kids might say—what matters

Is now—what is happening between us—
The kindness, the laughter, and the
Cherishing—I will have to pinch myself
For a long time to be entirely convinced

I didn't make you up, a figment of love.

Super Blue Blood Moon

You propose to me on the night
Of the super blue blood moon—
A celestial phenomenon which
Last occurred thirty-five years
Ago when we were first falling
In love—neither of us knew that
Then—but we have both become
Familiar with the cliché because
That is what has happened to us.

Ice Circles

Ice rims shimmer in circles on the reservoirs
I drive by early every morning—black water
Swirling underneath—this year the ice fishers

Are out—boring holes through glaciers—
Skaters swoop around them, giddy with this
Winter of freezing—it sleets and rains, snows

Before melting and then hardening all over again—
This winter snow lingers in mountains edging
Grocery store parking lots—the gray blending

In until it looks like smoke rings blown to
Pieces—we talk of global warming, or as some
Prefer to say, climate change—one of the wealthiest

Men on earth launches a rocket to mars, filled only
With a mannequin driving one of his spare red cars.

Ghost Nets

The package of plastic keeps growing—
Larger than seems humanly possible
To conceive—yet it is full of human

Refuse, plastic, discarded from ships
Large and small—ghost nets tossed
From large vessels trying to take fish

Without success—this glob of plastic
Is floating somewhere between
California and Hawaii—what my father

Used to call God's country—and now
We humans have tossed what we no
Longer desire—all the wrappings of our

Lives—thrown overboard or wasted
Into the ocean which we refuse to believe
Is neither infinite nor impermeable.

Notes from the Space Station

The woman who has spent the longest consecutive
Sequence of time in space—over six and a half months—
Sends in her report—as much as possible they tried

To replicate life on earth—Friday nights are for
Parties and whooping it up—learning how gravity
Lets everything fall away as soon as they entered

Orbit—nothing like the rush of blackness, she said—
Something she would miss—even though she
Recognizes that the spaceship shell had aged

Beyond safety—like an old 747 with all the ancient
Dials and knobs—how like and unlike life on earth
It was—most Saturdays they watched "Groundhog Day."

The Turkey and the Car, April

Yesterday morning I saw a wild turkey squished
Into the pavement—red blood and plumage mixed
Into a pigmented paint box of grit—caught on the

Bridge between two lakes crossing to the
Other side—later in the same day, deep into a
New England spring afternoon, the car in front

Of me swerved wildly—and came to a stop with
A turkey staring in the passenger seat window—
The car was halfway across the road, stuck

Sideways while the bird decided which way to
Go—and in the end, you could say the bird won
As the car backed up to let the turkey cross the
Road, threading her way through the greening bush.

Naming

I have been trying
For the longest time
To write a poem about you.

I get only this far.

How many images—
Cloudy afternoons,
October sunlight,
August noon
When the absence
Expands in love's
Presence.

We look through slotted blinds

At a moon, half full
In November rain.
Naming this twilight
Means leaving—

Only naming breaks us
From our objects,

So how could I possibly name you?

A Love Letter

And dreamt I saw you walking
In still warm sunlight
Covers rumpled, your sleepy
Eyes opening to find me.

This February light, its stillness
And sly delight, comes to
Search us out—like a sleek,
Gray cat—our wholeness.

And dreamt I saw you
Waking in still warm
Sunlight—this February light
Casts shadows infinite.

You are Here

In the dark, cold night
We share our touch and
Exploration—the shadow,
The act, the anticipation,
The caress.

The boundaries are laid,
Distances set—shivering,
I wonder—you catch my
Shiver—Yes, you are here,
You are here.

Response and action
Prelude and opus—
You are here.

Winter Song

Sing a song of these winter days,
Of quick mornings when lemon
Light slices our eyes, before the
Silent hum of routine, noontime
Brings sweet revenge and
Anonymity; tell of long
Afternoons with ideas rambling
When brief sun casts long and
Infinite, soft shadows across
These acres of fields.

Tell us quickly how night will
Come and bring respite from
Our restlessness; tell us how
Darkness will descend,
Providing us with our
Reflections and our doubts.
Others before have told us
Of these dancers—now, oh
Wise one, sing us these songs.

Ice Splinters

Submerged into glass splinters
Of ice, swimmers shivered in the
Fright of winter—later, in warmth
Of touch, their bodies would
Remember why they had broken
The barriers they used to know—
And the curved l in the word love
Would slide along the length
Of their touching tongues.

Geography

I learn Andover, the geography of greater
Lawrence, the various curves along Route
125—we no longer need a map—I learn
Other geography too—your face with its
Smiles, your solid chest—

I learn to drink wine in the afternoon,
Shadows form perfect circles of darkness.
It rains for a week—courtyards turn
Green—we come together for fires in the
Late afternoons, sunlight into leaf.

Letter from Oxford

I walk to the farthest postbox, as though to delay my
Decision—here in England, in this land of grandeur—
After disjointed thoughts, commands, tears that will
Not stop, long and silent meadow walks—I write

The sad letter to America—the missing has already
Begun—I do not understand then—I am far too young—
That only I hold the keys to my own life, listening to
Others has sent me far astray, it will take me a long

Time to reconstruct the love that settled in my heart—
I pick lilies of the valley to delay sorrow—sweetness
Cloys in memory—we have passed through the knowing
And the sadness—you will lie, a ghost at the back of

An attic I can't sweep—we made our days together—
Somewhere, we left children not conceived and laughter,
Accidents of love and understanding—a violent
Thunderstorm catches me unaware on the way home.

At the Charles Tomlinson Reading

She turns to make her whole—
He looks unassumingly into distance—
Quaint, she tips her head, blurred, his
Gaze lies beyond—daunted again, she
Stares out the window, to summer
Roses curled up, beneath passing clouds.

She cocks her head, in response, a quiet
Touching of her fingers, a nervous twitch
Perhaps—yes, he says with his legs and
Shifts his shoulders towards hers—she has
Made wholeness; she has won the contest
Of desire: their knees are touching.

Nether Winchendon

This village, this England, this
Afternoon smell of mowing and cattle—
Flies hum through the kitchen—cotton
Cloths protect the cakes waiting for tea.

Outside, there, the church stands with
Solemnity, making a pattern, a calendar
For people to live by—evensong, matins—
Who does the flowers now? Angela's in
A frightful row with Phyllis; where is the
Purple vase? No one would suspect this
Village of living in a nuclear age—wildflowers
Grow now over the crusaders' steps—the
Lady of the Manor protects her footpaths
With a shotgun.

This village, this England, this patch of
Green and certainty—holds the past in
Its arms.

At even hours, bells ring; next year they
Will mow spaces around the pillar box—
In the afternoon flies buzz.

I shell the peas.

July Requiem

Hot and late, the moon rises
Over grassy fields—like a child's
Cries, summer insects begin
Their chorus of voices and songs.
Summer sunshine fades with
Reluctance—days envelope
One another—nights seem
Short and light—sleeping
Vaguely, morning comes too soon.

But these summer mornings
Are all too quick—steps on
Terraces fade into stark noons—
Stopping to think, these July nights
Tell us of changes to come—summer
Will not stop, summer is not
Satisfied with satiation—the moon
Hangs on its threads, round and
Orbiting, it seems in no hurry
To close our days.

Wives Breakfasting at the Randolph Hotel*

Two painted faces stares out
Across a laid table, showing
Evenly the silver teapot
And the silent, cool knowing
Of their sex.

It is morning, a breakfast scene,
White cloths, flowing cream,
Flowers fading from a feast
The previous evening; the stream
Of light shades their faces.

One, slightly older, seems the
Leader, knowing all places,
She plans a day with
Pure routine.

In the knowing of their sex,
Following famous husbands
Through success, to reunions,
Adulations that impress,
Pride does not want more.

Men's departures seem routine
As diamond guard rings grow
Obscene—the fair sex make their lists,
Boutiques, cafes, and maybe rest,
As accoutrements to famous men,
Who never stop to ask when.

*Written on the occasion of the Rhodes Scholars reunion at Oxford; two of
their wives were breakfasting at the Randolph Hotel on the corner of St. Giles
and Beaumont Street.

October Sights

i

These are familiar sights:
The trees become sharp again—
A bent man rakes his life's
Property into gentle piles.
Orange pumpkins glow
From rows of bright colors
Along narrow roadways;
Darkness quickens on these
Early evenings.

ii

We all learn this season's
Shadows—we seek talismans
Of our rituals' arrivals—
Sweet smell of cider touches
The air—we make excursions
Along highways to ooh and sigh
At the beauty of unexpected
Contrasts stringing along
The winding roadsides.

iii

Children hide in fallen leaves—
They emerge with faces
Smudged with dust, scrapes
From small branches and
Twigs—happy with the
Knowledge of a beginning—
We are more sure of the
Changes to come—wintry
Light will soon darken our days.

iv

But for these bright spots,
For these days of respite
And reflection, joy and
Redemption, we are content with
Our present—we carve pumpkins,
Lighting candles to November.

Stars Cut into Darkening Skies

Someone once said you should not rerun memories—
Once lived, they should be left like a pile of old
Leaves too stiff too rake—on winter days even
The dog hesitates to press her paws into new snow—

When cold air freezes your breath, stars cut into
Darkening skies—cold air freezes ponds and heavy
Flakes burden hemlock trees—like long disappointments
Of failed promises, these boughs hang almost to the

Ground—once I thought there was a time for letting
Go—now I see a love that was always there
In that infinite moment when winter clears the air—

Memories awakening beneath a clearing sky.

Leaving Oxford on the Great Western Rail

Later afternoon on a train, leaving Oxford again, passing
Yellow fields, lilac hedgerows, May roses, querulous
Children arguing over a chocolate bar, a young woman

Sitting beside me with multiple piercings rolling her own
Cigarettes, clove perhaps, a distinct smell—my son sitting
Across from me—older now than I was when I first came

Here as a student—when I was young and inexperienced—
Impatient with the ways of adults, their dictums and mis-
Understandings—now we are delayed—as we were on

The way here—passing rivers, fields, I see it all anew through
Sunlight and tears—letter retracted, I whisper once or twice—

How one letter shaped two lives, how we have forgiven.

Postlude to a September Wedding

We walk to a clearing—green grass mowed for the occasion—
Only the remains of the party have been left to us—white
Tent raised, tablecloths on hangers, champagne glasses in dish

Trays ready for returning—a pile of ice chips dumped aside,
Sprinkled with lemon wedges—early Sunday morning when so
Many others are in church—yet we are here, seeing sunlight

On grass, nuptials passed—inside a young man is arranging
Chairs for his son's christening—and music lingers in the air—
If I close my eyes on this nippy fall morning, I can imagine

A bride and groom swaying together on a late August afternoon.

Heather Corbally Bryant is a Lecturer in the Writing Program at Wellesley College; previously she taught at Penn State University and Harvard College where she won awards for her teaching. She received her AB from Harvard and her PhD from the University of Michigan. Her first book, *How Will the Heart Endure: Elizabeth Bowen and the Landscape of War* (University of Michigan Press) won the Donald Murphy prize from the ACIS. She has published poems in *The Christian Science Monitor, Sixteen, The Paddock Review, Old Frog Pond Chapbooks, Fourth & Sycamore,* and in the anthologies: *In Another Voice, Open-Eyed, Full-Throated: An Anthology of American/Irish Poets* (Dublin: Arlen House, 2019) *Cheap Grace,* her first chapbook was published by Finishing Line Press. Her second collection of poems, *Lottery Ticket*, was published in 2013 by the Parallel Press Series of the University of Wisconsin Libraries-Madison. Her third chapbook, *Compass Rose*, appeared in 2015 from Finishing Line Press. *My Wedding Dress*, her first long collection of poems, was published by Finishing Line Press in 2016. *Thunderstorm*, her second full-length volume of poetry, was published by Finishing Line Press in the fall of 2017. It was nominated for a Mass Book Award in 2018. Her sixth collection of poetry, *Eve's Lament,* was published by Finishing Line Press in the winter of 2018. Her seventh collection of poetry, *James Joyce's Water Closet,* (2018) won honorable mention in the Open Chapbook Competition of the Finishing Line Press. Two of her poems, "James Joyce's Water Closet," and "The Easterly," were nominated for a Pushcart Prize in 2018. Her eighth collection of poetry, *Leaving Santorini*, appeared in 2018. She has given readings at colleges and bookstores across the United States, and in Ireland. She spends her summers in the Lakes Region of New Hampshire.

CPSIA information can be obtained
at www.ICGtesting.com
Printed in the USA
JSHW040933200720
6769JS00002B/79